Introducing Famous Americans

Meet George Washington

America's First President

Enslow Publishing
101 W. 23rd Street
Suite 240
New York, NY 10011
USA
enslow.com

Jane Katirgis and Tracie Egan

Published in 2020 by Enslow Publishing, LLC
101 W. 23rd Street, Suite 240, New York, NY 10011

Library of Congress Cataloging-in-Publication Data

Names: Katirgis, Jane, author. | Egan, Tracie, author.
Title: Meet George Washington : America's First President / Jane Katirgis and Tracie Egan.
Description: New York : Enslow Publishing, 2020. | Series: Introducing Famous Americans | Includes bibliographical references and index. | Audience: Grades 3–5.
Identifiers: LCCN 2018060038| ISBN 9781978511248 (library bound) | ISBN 9781978511224 (pbk.) | ISBN 9781978511231 (6 pack)
Subjects: LCSH: Washington, George, 1732–1799—Juvenile literature. | Presidents—United States—Biography—Juvenile literature.
Classification: LCC E312.66 .K37 2020 | DDC 973.4/1092 [B] —dc23
LC record available at https://lccn.loc.gov/2018060038

Printed in the United States of America

To Our Readers: We have done our best to make sure all website addresses in this book were active and appropriate when we went to press. However, the author and the publisher have no control over and assume no liability for the material available on those websites or on any websites they may link to. Any comments or suggestions can be sent by email to customerservice@enslow.com.

Portions of this book originally appeared in *George Washington: Father of the Nation*.

Photo Credits: Cover, p. 1 (Washington) SuperStock/Getty Images; cover, p. 1 (view of Mount Vernon) Everett/Shutterstock.com; pp. 5 (top), 18 (top) Library of Congress Geography and Map Division; p. 5 (bottom) Fine Art/Corbis Historical/Getty Images; pp. 6, 7, 26 (right) Courtesy of Mount Vernon Ladies' Association; pp. 8, 20, 22 (right), 24 Library of Congress Manuscript Division; p. 10 Courtesy National Gallery of Art, Washington, Andrew W. Mellon Collection; p. 11 Courtesy of National Museum of Dentistry, Baltimore, MD; p. 12 (top) Library of Congress; p. 12 (bottom) Private Collection/Peter Newark American Pictures/Bridgeman Images; p. 14 Library of Congress Rare Book and Special Collections Division; pp. 15 (top), 22 (left) Library of Congress Prints and Photographs Division; pp. 15 (bottom), 19, 25 New York Public Library Digital Collections; p. 16 National Center for the American Revolution/The Valley Forge Historical Society; pp. 17, 23 Bettmann/Getty Images; p. 18 (bottom) Courtesy of the George C. Neumann Collection, Valley Forge National Historic Park, photo by Cindy Reiman; p. 26 (left) Atlantisq/Shutterstock.com; interior pages background pattern and graphic elements Ambient Ideas/Shutterstock.com.

Contents

1 Fighting for Our Country

The people of America think of George Washington as the father of their country. During the Revolutionary War, George Washington led Americans to independence from England. He then became the first president of the United States.

Let's Learn More

During his life, George Washington received honorary degrees from Harvard, Yale, and Brown Universities. Today, these Ivy League schools are considered some of the best in America.

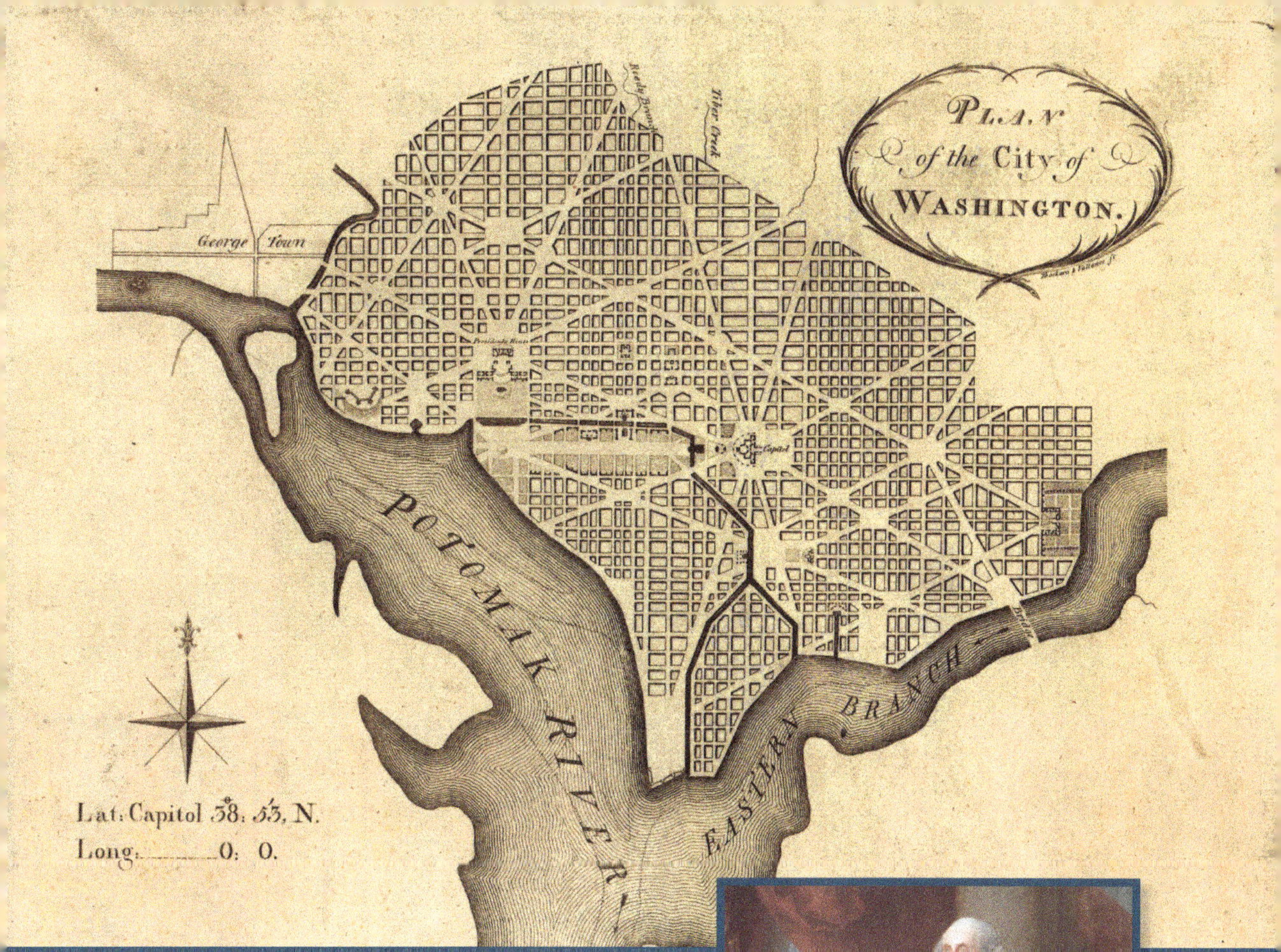

The map above shows an early plan for the new capital in Washington. At right is a portrait of George Washington by Gilbert Stuart.

In 1748, when Washington was 16 years old, he began working as a surveyor. Surveyors make maps and charts of unsettled land. Washington gained experience as a woodsman on his surveying trips.

When his older half brother Lawrence died, Washington inherited his plantation in Virginia. It was called Mount Vernon.

This painting shows Lawrence Washington, George Washington's older brother.

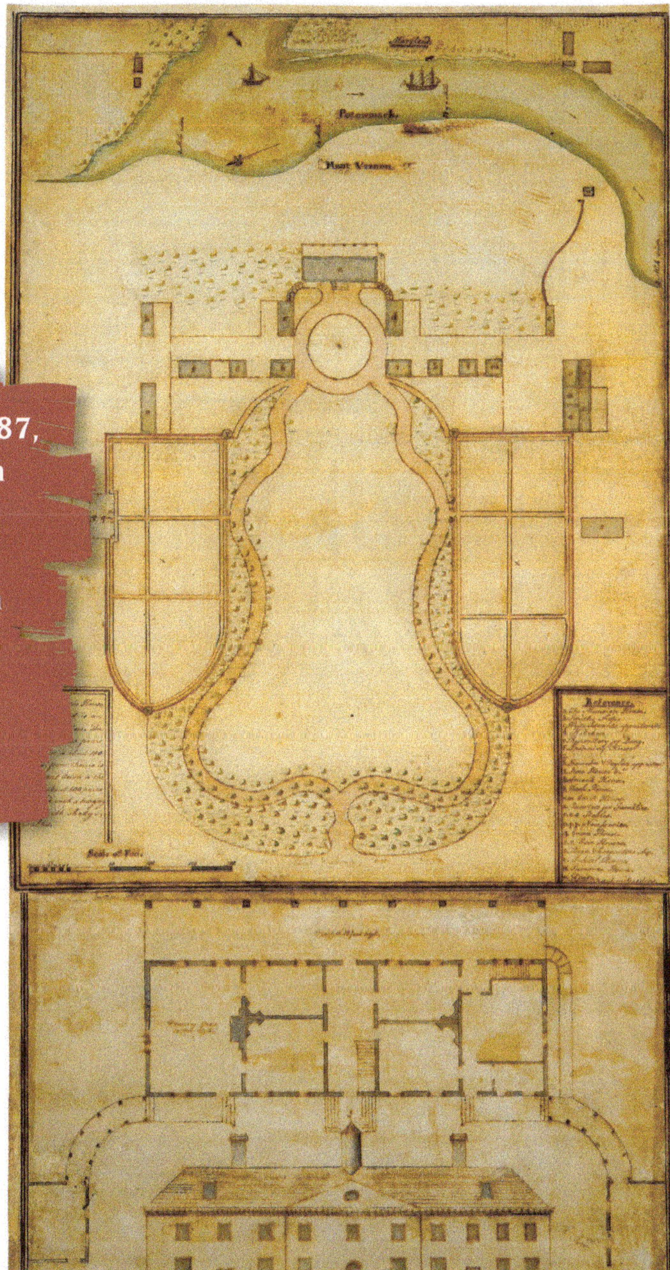

In November 1787, Samuel Vaughan drew and gave to Washington this ground plan of Washington's estate at Mount Vernon.

Washington took notes of his survey of a turnip field near Mount Vernon.

Washington joined the Virginia militia. In the militia he fought for the British, who ruled the American colonies. The militia battled the French for ownership of western lands in the French and Indian War.

In 1759, George Washington married Martha Dandridge Custis, a widow with two young children named Jacky and Patsy.

Let's Learn More

After fighting in the French and Indian War, Washington retired from the British army in 1758. It was as a soldier for the British that he learned military tactics and the skills of leadership.

When Washington married Martha Custis, he adopted her two children. This painting of the Washington family is by Edward Savage.

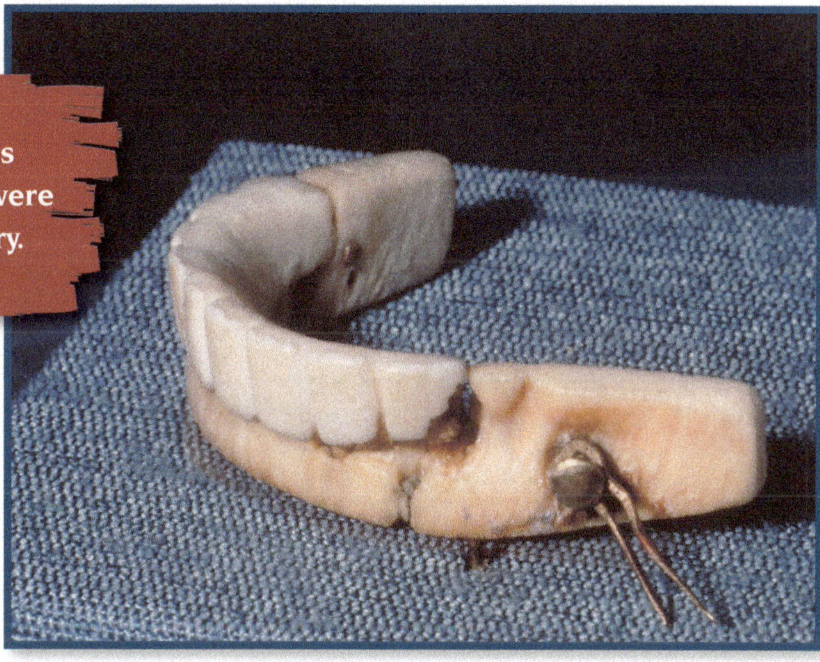

George Washington's false teeth were made of ivory.

The British government had many debts from its war with the French. To pay those debts, England imposed taxes on the American colonists. Many colonists believed it was unfair for England to tax them if they were not represented in the government. They were ready to fight for their independence.

Britain imposed a Stamp Act to tax all printed materials that had a stamp. A Pennsylvania newspaper suggested that the stamp be a skull and crossbones.

Washington wore the uniform of a colonial British colonel during the French and Indian War.

2 The Revolutionary War

The First Continental Congress took place in Philadelphia in September 1774. George Washington went as a representative from Virginia. He hoped to avoid war with England, but he did feel the British government was unjust.

Let's Learn More

Only about one-third of colonial Americans supported independence. One-third were neutral, and another third were Tory, or pro-British.

In 1774, the delegates of the First Continental Congress debated in Philadelphia whether to declare their independence from England.

On April 18, 1775, a group of British soldiers marched to Concord, Massachusetts, to seize the colonists' weapons. Paul Revere rode through the night, warning the colonists that the British were coming. At dawn on April 19, the first shot of the Revolutionary War was fired.

The Minutemen who responded to Paul Revere's midnight ride were mostly farmers.

British troops march through the town of Concord, Massachusetts. They suffered many losses and were driven back.

In June 1775, George Washington was appointed commander in chief of the American army. He thought his troops could fight the British in large battles. But in the summer of 1776, the Americans were defeated at Brooklyn Heights in a big battle. Washington decided upon a strategy of raiding and guerrilla warfare.

After their defeat at the Battle of Brooklyn, Washington and his troops retreat to Pennsylvania.

From his base in Pennsylvania, Washington made bold raids into New Jersey, harassing the British troops. Here, Washington and his troops cross the Delaware River.

On Christmas night in 1776, Washington and his troops crossed the Delaware River for a surprise attack on the British army the next day at Trenton, New Jersey. In one hour, the Americans captured almost 1,000 prisoners.

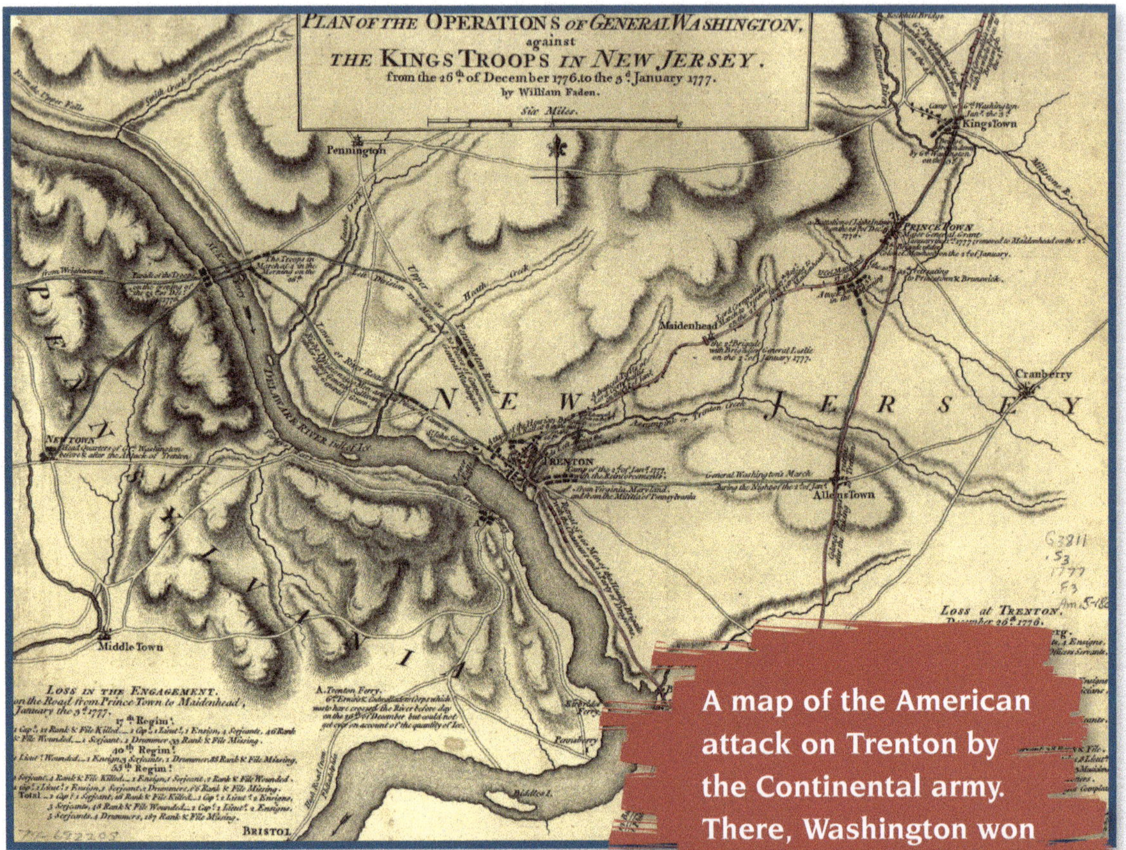

A map of the American attack on Trenton by the Continental army. There, Washington won an important victory.

Soldiers in the Continental army used this type of wooden canteen.

After years of fighting, the Americans surrounded British forces at Yorktown, Virginia. Here the British surrendered to Washington in 1781. The Americans had won the Revolutionary War.

In May 1787, Washington attended the Constitutional Convention in Philadelphia. Out of this convention came the US Constitution.

The Constitutional Convention in Philadelphia in 1787 drew up a new American constitution and created a strong federal government.

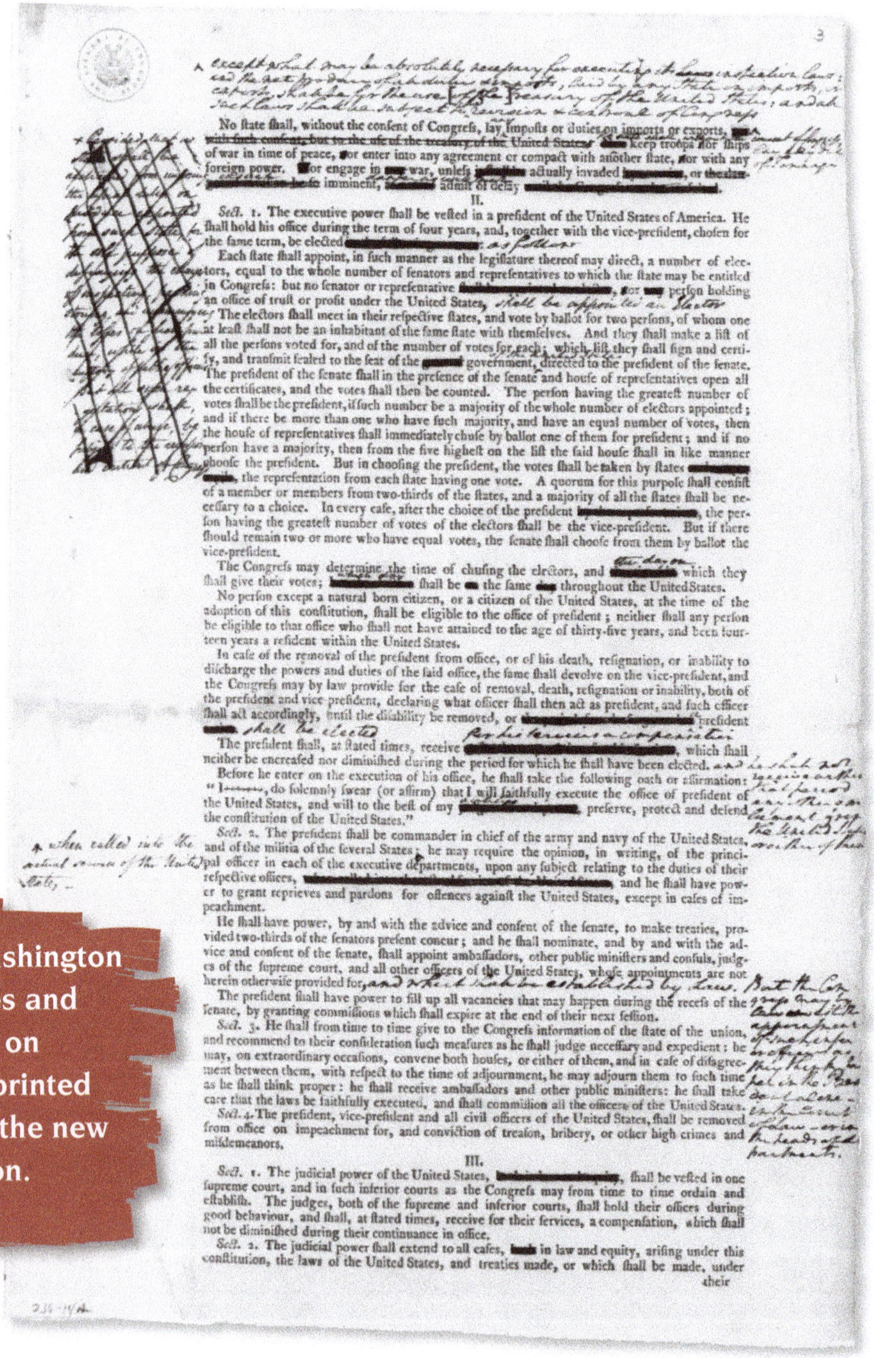

No state shall, without the consent of Congress, lay imposts or duties on imports or exports, keep troops or ships of war in time of peace, or enter into any agreement or compact with another state, or with any foreign power. or engage in war, unless actually invaded, or imminent, admit of delay

II.

Sect. 1. The executive power shall be vested in a president of the United States of America. He shall hold his office during the term of four years, and, together with the vice-president, chosen for the same term, be elected

Each state shall appoint, in such manner as the legislature thereof may direct, a number of electors, equal to the whole number of senators and representatives to which the state may be entitled in Congress: but no senator or representative, or person holding an office of trust or profit under the United States,

The electors shall meet in their respective states, and vote by ballot for two persons, of whom one at least shall not be an inhabitant of the same state with themselves. And they shall make a list of all the persons voted for, and of the number of votes for each; which list they shall sign and certify, and transmit sealed to the seat of the government, directed to the president of the senate. The president of the senate shall in the presence of the senate and house of representatives open all the certificates, and the votes shall then be counted. The person having the greatest number of votes shall be the president, if such number be a majority of the whole number of electors appointed; and if there be more than one who have such majority, and have an equal number of votes, then the house of representatives shall immediately chuse by ballot one of them for president; and if no person have a majority, then from the five highest on the list the said house shall in like manner choose the president. But in choosing the president, the votes shall be taken by states, the representation from each state having one vote. A quorum for this purpose shall consist of a member or members from two-thirds of the states, and a majority of all the states shall be necessary to a choice. In every case, after the choice of the president, the person having the greatest number of votes of the electors shall be the vice-president. But if there should remain two or more who have equal votes, the senate shall choose from them by ballot the vice-president.

The Congress may determine the time of chusing the electors, and which they shall give their votes; shall be the same throughout the United States.

No person except a natural born citizen, or a citizen of the United States, at the time of the adoption of this constitution, shall be eligible to the office of president; neither shall any person be eligible to that office who shall not have attained to the age of thirty-five years, and been fourteen years a resident within the United States.

In case of the removal of the president from office, or of his death, resignation, or inability to discharge the powers and duties of the said office, the same shall devolve on the vice-president, and the Congress may by law provide for the case of removal, death, resignation or inability, both of the president and vice president, declaring what officer shall then act as president, and such officer shall act accordingly, until the disability be removed, or president

The president shall, at stated times, receive, which shall neither be encreased nor diminished during the period for which he shall have been elected.

Before he enter on the execution of his office, he shall take the following oath or affirmation: "I ——, do solemnly swear (or affirm) that I will faithfully execute the office of president of the United States, and will to the best of my preserve, protect and defend the constitution of the United States."

Sect. 2. The president shall be commander in chief of the army and navy of the United States, and of the militia of the several States; he may require the opinion, in writing, of the principal officer in each of the executive departments, upon any subject relating to the duties of their respective offices, and he shall have power to grant reprieves and pardons for offences against the United States, except in cases of impeachment.

He shall have power, by and with the advice and consent of the senate, to make treaties, provided two-thirds of the senators present concur; and he shall nominate, and by and with the advice and consent of the senate, shall appoint ambassadors, other public ministers and consuls, judges of the supreme court, and all other officers of the United States, whose appointments are not herein otherwise provided for,

The president shall have power to fill up all vacancies that may happen during the recess of the senate, by granting commissions which shall expire at the end of their next session.

Sect. 3. He shall from time to time give to the Congress information of the state of the union, and recommend to their consideration such measures as he shall judge necessary and expedient: he may, on extraordinary occasions, convene both houses, or either of them, and in case of disagreement between them, with respect to the time of adjournment, he may adjourn them to such time as he shall think proper: he shall receive ambassadors and other public ministers: he shall take care that the laws be faithfully executed, and shall commission all the officers of the United States.

Sect. 4. The president, vice-president and all civil officers of the United States, shall be removed from office on impeachment for, and conviction of treason, bribery, or other high crimes and misdemeanors.

III.

Sect. 1. The judicial power of the United States, shall be vested in one supreme court, and in such inferior courts as the Congress may from time to time ordain and establish. The judges, both of the supreme and inferior courts, shall hold their offices during good behaviour, and shall, at stated times, receive for their services, a compensation, which shall not be diminished during their continuance in office.

Sect. 2. The judicial power shall extend to all cases, in law and equity, arising under this constitution, the laws of the United States, and treaties made, or which shall be made, under their

George Washington wrote notes and comments on this early printed version of the new Constitution.

3 Our First President

It was time for the people to choose their first president. When the votes in the new electoral college were counted, George Washington had received all of them. John Adams was elected vice president. George Washington was sworn in as the first president of the United States on April 30, 1789.

Let's Learn More

Election of the president by electoral college was a political compromise so that states with large numbers of free citizens would not dominate the government.

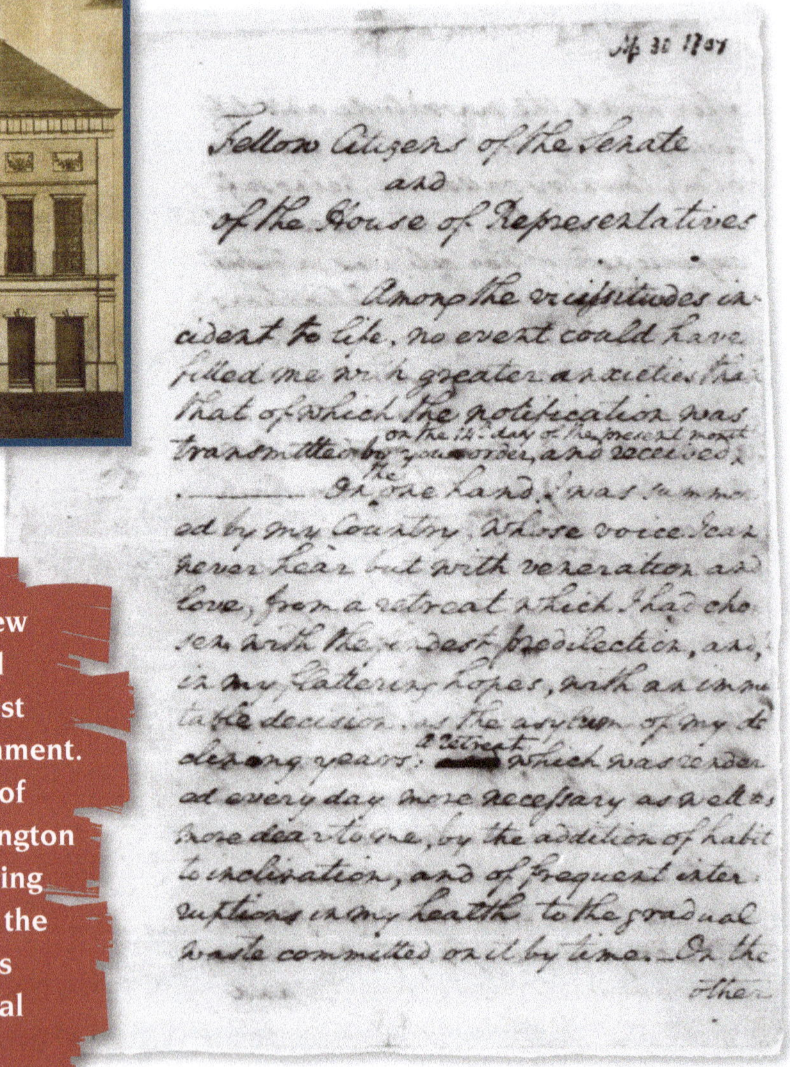

Ap 30 1789

Fellow Citizens of the Senate
and
of the House of Representatives

Among the vicissitudes incident to life, no event could have filled me with greater anxieties than that of which the notification was transmitted by your order, and received on the 14th day of the present month. On the one hand, I was summoned by my Country, whose voice I can never hear but with veneration and love, from a retreat which I had chosen with the fondest predilection, and, in my flattering hopes, with an immutable decision, as the asylum of my declining years: a retreat which was rendered every day more necessary as well as more dear to me, by the addition of habit to inclination, and of frequent interruptions in my health to the gradual waste committed on it by time. On the other

Federal Hall in New York City, pictured above, was the first seat of the government. At right is a copy of the speech Washington gave upon accepting the presidency of the United States. It is called an inaugural address.

One of President Washington's first tasks was to create departments within the government. Washington created the Departments of War, Treasury, and State. Henry Knox was made secretary of war. Alexander Hamilton became secretary of the treasury. Thomas Jefferson was appointed secretary of state.

Washington's cabinet included Secretary of State Thomas Jefferson, who is seated second from the right.

At the end of his term, Washington did not want to serve as president again. But when the votes were counted, he was elected again. In 1797, George Washington finally retired as president.

In his farewell address, Washington advised Americans to avoid permanent alliances and to avoid political factions at home.

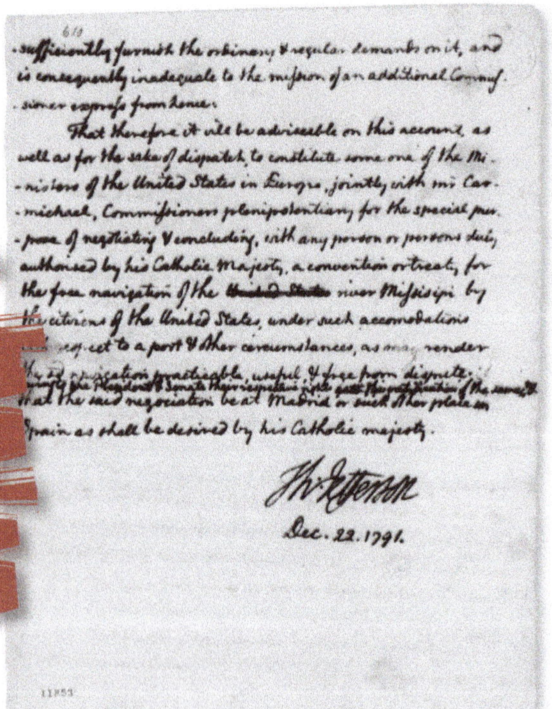

sufficiently furnish the ordinary & regular demands on it, and
is consequently inadequate to the mission of an additional Commis-
sioner express from home.

That therefore it will be adviseable on this account, as
well as for the sake of dispatch, to constitute some one of the Mi-
nisters of the United States in Europe, jointly with mr Car-
michael, Commissioners plenipotentiary for the special pur-
pose of negotiating & concluding, with any person or persons duly
authorised by his Catholic Majesty, a convention or treaty for
the free navigation of the river Missisipi by
the citizens of the United States, under such accomodations
with respect to a port & other circumstances, as may render
the said navigation practicable, useful, & free from dispute;
[illegible]
that the said negociation be at Madrid or such other place in
Spain as shall be desired by his Catholic majesty.

Th: Jefferson
Dec. 22. 1791.

Jefferson wrote this document while he was secretary of state. His arguments with Hamilton caused Washington to hate political factions.

This is a copy of Washington's farewell address to the nation after serving two terms as president.

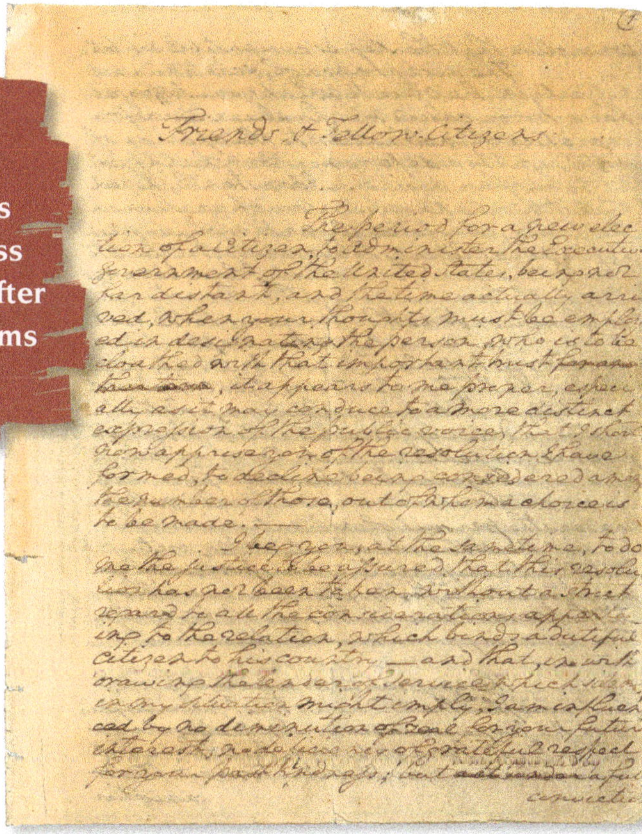

Friends & Fellow Citizens.

The period for a new election of a Citizen, to administer the Executive government of the United States, being not far distant, and the time actually arrived, when your thoughts must be employed in designating the person, who is to be clothed with that important trust for another term, it appears to me proper, especially as it may conduce to a more distinct expression of the public voice, that I should now apprize you of the resolution I have formed, to decline being considered among the number of those, out of whom a choice is to be made.—

I beg you, at the same time, to do me the justice to be assured, that this resolution has not been taken, without a strict regard to all the considerations appertaining to the relation, which binds a dutiful citizen to his country—and that, in withdrawing the tender of service which silence in my situation might imply, I am influenced by no diminution of zeal for your future interest, no deficiency of grateful respect for your past kindness; but am supported by a full convictio[n]

Let's Learn More

Legend has it that George Washington had wooden teeth. Actually, he had dentures made of different materials, including hippopotamus ivory, cows' teeth, and metal.

Washington was happy to go home to Mount Vernon. In December 1799, he caught a throat infection while riding his horse in the harsh winter weather. On December 14, 1799, he died at home in his bed. He was 67 years old.

This statue of George Washington on horseback stands in the Public Garden next to Boston Common in Boston, Massachusetts.

This engraving shows George Washington on his deathbed. In the eighteenth century, simple infections could be fatal.

Timeline

1732 – George Washington is born.

1748 – Washington becomes a surveyor at age 16.

1759 – Washington marries Martha Dandridge Custis.

1774 – In September, Washington attends the First Continental Congress in Philadelphia as a representative of Virginia.

1775 – On April 19, the first shot of the Revolutionary War is fired in Massachusetts; in June, Washington is appointed commander in chief of the Continental army.

1776 – On July 4, Congress approves the Declaration of Independence; on Christmas night, Washington and his troops cross the Delaware River for a surprise attack on British troops.

1781 – In October, the British surrender at Yorktown.

1783 – In December, Washington retires from the military.

1789 – On April 30, Washington is sworn in as the first president of the United States.

1797 – Washington retires as president. Vice President John Adams is elected as the second president of the United States.

1799 – In December, Washington catches a throat infection. He dies at the age of 67.

Glossary

colony (KAH-luh-nee) A settlement in a new country that is still controlled by another country.

debt (DET) Something owed.

declaration (deh-kluh-RAY-shun) A formal statement.

militia (muh-LIH-shuh) A group of citizens who are trained to fight but who serve only in a time of emergency.

plantation (plan-TAY-shun) A very large farm where crops are grown.

representative (reh-prih-ZEN-tuh-tiv) An elected spokesperson for a group of people.

surrender (suh-REN-dur) To admit defeat to the enemy and lay down arms.

taxes (TAKS-ez) Money the government takes from citizens to pay its expenses.

widow (WIH-doh) A woman whose husband has died.

Learn More

Books

Demuth, Patricia. *What Is the Constitution?* New York, NY: Penguin Workshop, 2018.

Meltzer, Brad. *I Am George Washington*. New York, NY: Dial Books for Young Readers, 2016.

Van Lente, Fred. *Action Presidents #1: George Washington!*. New York, NY: HarperCollins, 2018.

Websites

George Washington's Mount Vernon

mountvernon.org/education/for-students

Learn more about George Washington and the era in which he lived.

National Geographic

kids.nationalgeographic.com/explore/history/presidential-fun-facts

Provides fun facts about US presidents.

Social Studies for Kids

socialstudiesforkids.com/articles/ushistory/presidentialelections1.htm

Read about the history of presidential elections in the United States.

Primary Source Image List

Page 5: Top: Plan of the City of Washington by Pierre Charles L'Enfant, Philadelphia, 1792, now with the Library of Congress. Bottom: Portrait of George Washington by Gilbert Stuart, 1792.

Page 6: Lawrence Washington, painted by John Wollaston in 1738, oil on canvas.

Page 7: Ground plan of Mount Vernon by Samuel Vaughan, 1787.

Page 8: From George Washington's second school copy book, 1747/1748.

Page 10: *The Washington Family* by Edward Savage, oil on canvas, 1796.

Page 12: Top: Woodcut from the *Pennsylvania Journal and Weekly Advertiser*. Bottom: Portrait of George Washington as a colonial British officer, by Charles Wilson Peale, oil on canvas, 1772.

Page 14: *Premiere assemblée du congrès*, an engraving by François Godefoy, 1782.

Page 15: Bottom: A *View of the Town of Concord*, engraved in 1775 by Sidney L. Smith after a painting by Amos Doolittle.

Primary Source Image List

Page 17: *Plan of the operations of General Washington, against the Kings troops in New Jersey, from the 26th, of December, 1776, to the 3d. January 1777*, by William Faden. Printed in London, 1777.

Page 20: Draft of the Constitution with Washington's handwritten annotations.

Page 22: Right: Handwritten draft of George Washington's first inaugural address, delivered to Congress at Federal Hall in New York City, 1789.

Page 24: Letter from Thomas Jefferson to George Washington, December 22, 1791.

Page 25: Final draft of George Washington's Farewell Address, 1796.

Page 26: Right: *George Washington in His Last Illness Attended by Doctors Craik and Brown*. Etching by an unidentified artist, early 19th century.

Index